THE PLAN UNDER PRESSURE

THE COUNCIL FOR
ECONOMIC EDUCATION, BOMBAY

THE PLAN UNDER PRESSURE

An Observer's View

by

BARBARA WARD

ASIA PUBLISHING HOUSE — LONDON

PRINTED IN INDIA

BY D. C. PATOLE AT THE HIND PRESS, BOMBAY,
AND PUBLISHED BY P. S. JAYASINGHE, ASIA
PUBLISHING HOUSE, 447, STRAND, LONDON W.C. 2

INTRODUCTION

In the series of lectures on India's current economic problems which the Council for Economic Education organises from time to time, Lady Jackson delivered this December two lectures on "The Plan Under Pressure—An Observer's View," at Jai Hind College, Bombay. Both the lectures attracted large audiences and proved extremely popular. In keeping with the practice of the Council, the lectures are now being published for the benefit of a larger public.

Lady Jackson, or Barbara Ward as she is so familiarly known, needs no introduction to the Indian public. Even before India appointed official economic ambassadors, she through her writings and lectures, had virtually served us as our economic ambassador to the West. In fact, her book, *India and the West,* contains most of the arguments that one might seek to advance in favour of maximum economic assistance to India.

It is because her approach to India's economic problems has been as sympathetic as it has been analytical that Lady Jackson's views on the Plan acquire a special significance. Under the modest sub-title "An Observer's View" she covers a wide range of economic topics and puts across a number of suggestions which are thought-provoking.

Starting with a review of the variety of pressures to which Indian economy was exposed when the Chinese advanced on the country in mid-October, Lady Jackson refers to the likely impact of defence mobilisation on industrial production and stresses the desirability of an agreed solution of the Kashmir question—a political issue—for facilitating the flow of Western aid. In the context of foreign aid she has a few pertinent observations to make on the level of tariffs imposed by the developed countries on the products of the developing countries and of the attitude of the latter to foreign private investment. She argues that, provided certain conditions are fulfilled,

Britain's entry into the European Common Market—no longer a live issue—will be to the advantage of the developing countries. She lays great emphasis on the need of India developing her forest wealth and evolving a pattern of technology suitable to her resources.

Lady Jackson believes that the time has come for India to evaluate the accounting significance of prices, not only in the narrow sense of prices of commodities but also of prices of capital (rate of interest), foreign exchange (rate of exchange), etc. To the extent that these prices are not indicative of their real value, they lead to a wasteful use of the scarce factors of production.

It is hoped that these views of a keen observer will stimulate fresh thinking on our economic problems and suggest new lines of action.

CONTENTS

1. The Immediate Crisis 1

2. Planning for Growth 26

3. The Foreign Exchange Crisis 48

1

The Immediate Crisis

The subject to which I have to address myself—"The Plan under Pressure"—is about the most difficult subject that one could choose at this time. Can one say what the future shape of the Plan is going to be? Can one define the likely scale of the pressure? If I feel rather like the proverbial man in a dark room groping for a dark cat, you must forgive me. The subject is immensely tenuous and every time one thinks to lay hold on an absolutely solid fact, the fact either dissolves or turns into something quite different.

Even our starting point—the emergency itself—is a very uncertain affair, once we leave the brute fact of aggression. Is it a prelude to all-out war? Or pressure designed to bring India back to the negotiating table in a more compliant frame of mind? Or opportunism, part of a long process of probing here and probing there, weakening the independence of border states, undermining India's status and self-respect and reducing the Himalayas from a secure frontier to a threatened no-man's land? Having no direct insight into Mao Tse-tung's thinking, we can only guess and all I can tell is that the most informed guesses these days seem to conclude that India is faced with one of the most unpleasant and most difficult kinds of conflict a nation can be compelled to face—a sort of "on-again, off-again Flanagan" conflict, in which the enemy never gives its opponents for any length of time, the brisk, invigorating sense of open struggle, but continuously saps away at the foundations of their essential interests and of their long-term defence.

What happened in October-November, 1962, certainly fits into this picture. Indian troops, the Chinese alleged, were probing forward in Ladakh, part of which the Chinese are determined to keep. Now, the Chinese could, I suppose, in these conditions have responded solely in Ladakh, delivering a very strong attack there to bring their frontier within sight of Chusul. What did they do? They chose instead by a surprise attack in NEFA to deal a devastating blow at the Indian Army and hence at Indian prestige. Here was the demonstration that, when it comes to *power*, there is at this moment only one effective power system inside Asia—the Chinese system.

It served notice on the Indian people that their frontiers are very largely defenceless. And it reminded them of how vulnerable the lands behind the Himalayan frontier really are. I doubt whether aggression in Ladakh could have illustrated this point so clearly since the loss of Ladakh would not open the great river plains of India to direct attack. I do not, of course, mean to suggest that the Ladakh aggression can be simply swallowed. India's reaction has been entirely sane since nothing is more dangerous than that any great nation should acquire the sense that it can take what it likes from its neighbours' territory. This attitude is one to be discouraged from a very early stage of the game. But in NEFA, the issue is more than one of discouraging aggression. Look at Assam, study the map of that corner of India and you will see that it is the intersecting point of half a dozen states, all vulnerable, some at odds with each other, most of them open to Chinese pressure. And behind NEFA, any renewed drive could carry the enemy into the tea gardens of Assam and with their loss would go nearly 20 per cent of India's foreign exchange earnings—already grossly inadequate to the tasks facing the Indian economy.

In short, the Chinese, by striking in NEFA, have certainly exposed much more immediate and crucial interests than any at issue in Ladakh. Ladakh touches, of course, on national prestige. When, however, the issue at stake is an essential element of a nation's economy and beyond that, the survival in security of vital, developed industrial regions—one thinks of the vulnerability of West Bengal and Bihar—then clearly the Chinese have served notice on India that its vital interests are at the moment wholly unprotected. Whether the Chinese have withdrawn for good, or for a time, or only until the spring, the grim fact remains that, so long as the present Indian defensive posture remains unchanged, India is undefended.

The fact that the Chinese have made the demonstration so brutally could turn out to be their gravest error. If a nation intends a long spell of expansion, it would be well advised to go about it quietly at the start. Of course, the Chinese consider power a perfectly legitimate weapon for dealing with people with less power. But their neighbours were perhaps not fully aware of the fact. Now, the violent warning they have given cannot be disregarded and perhaps it could not have been hammered home in any less brutal way. Was this a lesson they really wanted to teach so soon?

The openness of the aggression is the first reason for supposing that Chinese aggressiveness cannot be simply wished away by appealing to Panch Sheel or Asian solidarity. Nor do Chinese withdrawals point in a different direction. It is a well-known trick in ju-jitsu to give your opponent a blow, brace yourself to receive his counter-blow, then when he launches it, fall back and allow his own weight to bring him down. The basic fact remains that the Chinese have the power to come and go as they choose.

What they will choose is, as I have remarked, locked in the brain of China's leaders. But we have some ominous pointers which should not be ignored. To restore the sovereignty of Peking over lands once owing it allegiance is a recurrent aim of new Chinese dynasties—and the Communists are in a real sense a reincarnation of the old dynasties thrown up by popular despair and led by peasants. Such an aim involves a very extensive potential enlargement of Chinese control.

Quite apart from states such as Viet Nam which were once part of the Chinese system, a further vague penumbra of states could be included. Often, in times gone by, when harmless ambassadors arrived in Peking and, as was the custom of the time, gave his celestial majesty a present, his celestial majesty, with his profound contempt for everyone outside the "Middle Kingdom," simply assumed that, as "barbarians," they were naturally paying tribute and accepting vassal status. On this interpretation, Burma, Nepal, Bhutan, possibly Assam and even states as remote as Indonesia, could be reckoned part of the Chinese area of predominance. Now, if all these states come, as it were, to be "gathered in," India would be confronted with an overwhelming concentration of power and one which would have altered the balance of power in the world in a formidable sense.

It is these larger ambitions and possibilities which make it impossible for India simply to accept the current Chinese withdrawal as equivalent to the removal of danger. The Chinese have gone. They can come back. They have historical and imperial reasons for doing so. Therefore, the only sane thing for India to do is to buy time. The mistake must not be made, as was made by Mr. Chamberlain at Munich, to believe that, because something turned out to be not quite so bad as he had feared, he had bought peace. Actually, the British did do something with that bit of time between 1938 and 1939; they bought Spitfires. But in general one can say that during that year, from Munich to the outbreak of war, we did not buy enough. Today India may be going to be given time. The essential thing is to concentrate on "buying" a frontier that is defensible and a military system that can defend it.

Let us look first at the military side—the problem of mounting an effective defence force capable of seeing that, the next time the Chinese try a probe in NEFA, it is they who get the shock. Now, I am not Major Barbara, I cannot put on my strategist's hat at this stage. All I can say is that there does seem to be a certain concurrence of military opinion that to restore a proper posture of effective defence on the northern frontiers India would need to envisage a doubling of the present defence establishment and a considerable modernization of arms and equipment. And equally there seems to be broad agreement that such an effort would not cost less than Rs. 450 to 500 crores over the next twelve months.

If we accept this as a reasonable estimate, we can begin to measure its impact on the Indian economy. And there is no disguising the fact that the emergency overcame India at a time of very considerable economic strain. Let us look at the position as it was in August 1962. At that time, it was already clear that the Third Plan was running into some very real difficulties. In the course of 1961 and 1962, the general growth of the Indian economy had been disappointing. To reach the targets of the Third Plan, an annual rate of growth in national income of the order of at least 5 per cent had been forecast. Instead of that, growth barely reached 3 per cent and, with a population increase of about 2 per cent, there was clearly very little margin left for further investment or rise in consumption—and very little margin for satisfaction either. To find India's rate of growth among the lowest in Asia—a fact brought out in a recent UN Report—was an unpleasant shock.

The various reasons for this slow-down do, I think, point to some of the pressures that were at work on the Plan even before the emergency arose. First of all, we must look at the disappointing performance in agriculture. The hope had been to secure an annual rise of 6 per cent in farm production; instead, in 1961/62 the level was just under 2 per cent. This relatively unsatisfactory performance had something to do, as usual, with the weather. But it had more to do with the fact that reform and reorganization in agriculture were proving slower and more complicated than the planners had hoped. Existing channels still fail to get to the farmer the fertiliser, the improved seed, the insecticide and so forth that he needs either in sufficient quantity or on time. One particularly critical aspect of this widespread failure to meet farming targets can be seen in the field of irrigation. Here, after all, is the chance to achieve complete independence of the weather. The target for increased irrigation—both major and minor—in the Third Plan is something like 26 million acres. Yet, in 1961/62, only about 3 million acres of fresh land were brought under irrigation. If this figure were projected, it would mean that not much more than half of the Plan's final target would be achieved. Nor are agricultural delays significant only for farming. Industry, too, has been affected by the fall in cotton production from 5.4 million bales to 4.5 million and the failure of oil seeds to grow in any significant way. Table 1 gives some of the key figures.

TABLE 1

	1960/61	*1961/62*	*Target 1965/66*
Cereals (m. tons)	67.5	67.2	83
Oilseeds (m. tons)	6.5	6.8	9.8
Sugar cane (m. tons)	10.4	9.7	10
Cotton (m. bales)	5.4	4.5	7
Jute (m. bales)	4.0	6.3	6.2

Source: Official Statistics.

In fact, one must go further and underline the degree to which, in an economy still so near the edge of subsistence, agriculture tends to condition the whole performance of the economy. The fact is not surprising. Some 70 per cent of India's peoples live on the land. Nearly 80 per cent of its crucial export earnings depend, directly or indirectly, upon the countryside. Above all, in any time of inflationary strain, it is the country's food supplies that will determine whether or not the strain can be carried without catastrophe. People living near the margin will always spend almost the whole of any increase in income on food. Between 1958 and 1961 the output of food grains grew by about 12 per cent. But the number of people grew by about the same percentage. Releases of American food reserves have helped to offset sudden fluctuations. Yet the upward pressure on prices has not ceased. In 1962, the increase in the wholesale price of food was as much as 11 per cent. Even before the emergency, the margins looked very narrow.

However, before turning to the industrial record, I think this is the point at which to underline one fact. Any criticism, any pointing to shortcomings must be placed in the proper context — and in India, this context *is* one of sustained growth. The growth may not be as high as the planners would wish but, before the advent of the Plans, India's economy had been either stationary or regressive for at least twenty or thirty years. The spurts of industrial growth of both world wars had been offset by political confusion or economic stagnation or both. In agriculture, the failure was worse for, in 1947, India inherited a farming system which, caught between rising population, rigid landowning and tenancy systems, growing fragmentation and lowered productivity, led, decade after decade, to a fall in per capita consumption. Independent India inherited the typical framework of a post-colonial economy—development, infrastructure and cities largely centred on the export sectors, a relatively small educated élite, little industrial development, and stagnant agriculture — and although it was better than the norm in some cases. for instance. in education, administrative talents, a railway network and some lively indigenous business groups, it was worse off in the pressure of population on the land and the long stagnation of agriculture.

Given this background, it has been a Herculean task to swing the whole vast system out of its stationary mould and into the ways of growth — growth in every sector, growth which is ahead of the population and growth which, it is not unreasonable to hope, can lead, at last, to settled growth which sustains itself without exceptional, outside assistance. Therefore, when the critics pick out things that are not going as they would wish, it is not to say that there is not, underlying the whole of the economy, a new surge of growth. It would be ridiculous to forget it.

It would be equally unwise not to look at the areas of pressure. In 1961/62, the industrial record, apart from textiles, was not too far behind the 8-10 per cent average of the earlier Plans, but it was pulled down by a bad year in cotton to about 5 per cent. Here we meet straightaway the essential interdependence of farming and industry and this is a point that one has to underline over and over again. In all developing countries, the health of the land determines almost everything else. This is not to say that industrial growth is secondary. On the contrary, it is the way ahead — but the launching pad is agriculture. No sane man questions India's need of industry—including heavy industry. In a country with the resources possessed by India, with massive supplies of iron ore, with reasonably good supplies of coking coal and a fine potential in hydro-electricity, it makes every kind of sense to have a steel industry. One must not be misled by starry-eyed back-to-the-landers who tell you that any developing country which wants a steel mill is behaving in an irrational way. On the contrary, the Indian pattern of concentration on the building up of its steel industry and of its mechanical industries makes perfect sense in view of its resources and the scale of its internal market. The emphasis here is simply designed to counter any tendency to obsession with steel mills to the exclusion of other essential things.

Every now and then when people turn with gleaming eyes to look at a steel mill, they forget that steel is just one small part of an advance on the whole industrial sector; in point of fact, at this stage they ought to look with eyes that gleam no less at any really perfectly cultivated field of cotton or jute or groundnuts. A smoking factory chimney should not be more of a status-symbol than the efficient seed farm by which Indian standards of productivity can begin to reach world levels. It is a fact that Indian cotton output is, on the average, only about 90 lbs. an acre. Yet it is 540 lbs. an acre in Egypt and, even in Pakistan, the average has gone up to 230 lbs. India's low productivity menaces its industrial as well as its agricultural growth. So let us keep the balance of our enthusiasm and let us not only look at steel mills as the "cathedrals of the future" but also remember that a great deal of proper devotion should be dedicated to the economy's more modest performers and that a fine fertile field of cotton is one of the great supports of rapid industrial growth. The experience of 1961/62 underlines this point very vividly since the check to the industrial rate of growth sprang precisely from a shortfall in cotton.

This absolute dependence of industry and, indeed, the whole economy, upon a vital, growing, well-organised and fruitful agricultural sector is something which all developing countries, and India in particular, have to bear in mind. There must be no snobbism in favour of industry, and no idea that some forms of output are more "chic" than others. The only really "chic" form of economic activity is the one that will give you a steady return of 10 per cent on your investment. If farming, industry and services are all reaching that level, savings will appear, further investment will be possible and more growth will result.

Other elements in the slow-down are, of course, quite familiar. They amount to a series of interlocking bottlenecks at the base of the economy. Steel has been slow to expand. Coal production—at about 55 million tons—has disappointingly remained at almost exactly the same level as 1961. Then there are transport problems. The wagon-dispatching system has not proved adequate to keep the coal moving to the power plants and the steel mills. Nor has it kept the end products moving away steadily from the plants. And, although the evidence likely to be given on the subject by a steel man may be different from that of a railway man, there is a general belief that the turn-round time in the marshalling yards could certainly be shortened.

And all these interlocking difficulties hit back to the crucial element of power. Certainly, power production is increasing in India. During the Second Plan, power capacity nearly doubled — to 5.7 million kilowatts. It is to double again by 1965. Yet it is apparently a law of life in economies that, once a projection of power demand has been made, it should be increased by at least one-third; and even then shortages are likely, because a growing economy is so voracious of power that it is practically impossible to over-estimate the need for it. You may get local pockets of over-production of power when you plan, for example, a power station with a particular purpose, for instance, to serve an aluminium plant, and the aluminium plant is not ready on time. But in general, even the best conceived power system is bound to be under strain in periods of growth. But in India severe interruptions in the supply of coal have added to the strain and have led to widespread dislocations and even shut-downs in industry.

At this point I want to leave the internal difficulties and turn to the most serious of all the shortages plaguing the Indian economy — the shortage of foreign exchange. It is not entirely new. In 1957/58 there was a similar crisis in foreign exchange because, in both Plans, there seems to have been a similar difficulty in forecasting the scale of foreign exchange likely to be demanded by an economy which is growing steadily along a wide front. In 1958, the shortages led first to severe cuts in the core of the Plan. Some of them—notably in coal washeries and power capacity—have been of a disturbing element ever since. Yet the crisis did lead to the forming of an Aid-India Consortium of Western nations which has been on the job ever since and contrived between 1958 and 1961 to make available about $2000 million in outside aid.

Now, however, in spite of commitments to the Third Plan of the order of $1000 million a year, new stresses have appeared. The scale of the crisis is not entirely clear. At the moment, Indian exports seem to stick fast at a level of about Rs. 600 crores while imports remain above Rs. 900 crores. Exports barely increased in 1962 — but the various policies induced to increase exports have not yet had much effect. Perhaps they were introduced too recently to expect any very big result. Nor is the climate for exports in the international market all that it should be. There is an element here quite certainly beyond India's control. The steady decline, relatively speaking, in the prices of primary materials, the competitiveness of Asian manufactured exports, the great uncertainty introduced by the Common Market negotiations—all these have a depressing effect upon any developing country's ability to earn large increases in foreign exchange.

Most of these difficulties lie outside the control of the Indian government. But there is one point over which both India's planners and the members of the Consortium have perhaps not been sufficiently clear-sighted. Have they sufficiently measured the amount of foreign exchange, in terms of maintenance imports and of raw materials, which a functioning economy inevitably requires? So much of the planning of projects and the general expansion of capacity appears almost to have assumed that the foreign exchange needed for running the projects would follow from the general development of the economy. In point of fact, what does emerge — and at once — is a steadily growing strain on foreign exchange. By the middle of 1962 — as in 1957 — it was quite apparent that some of the calculations of the Plan would have to be very drastically revised. Between 1960 and the middle of 1962, the revision of foreign exchange requirements uncovered by exports or foreign investment has gone steadily upwards from about Rs. 2,000 crores up to some Rs. 3,000 crores. At this point, it became apparent that, although the Aid-India Club was probably likely to maintain its aid at the level of about a billion dollars a year — or 5 billions over the five years of the Plan — the revisions were leading to requirements that would be nearer $7.5 billion. Of such an increase, there was absolutely no sign at all.

So, in the course of the summer of 1962, the need came to be more and more keenly felt to re-tailor the Plan to the flow of foreign exchange that would be likely to be available. While, however, this whole re-consideration of the Plan was going on, the emergency supervened and all the planning and reckoning had to begin again from a new starting point—the impact of the emergency.

Such, then, was the condition of stress and strain in the Indian economy when, in October 1962, the Chinese launched their attack and put the Indian people on notice that nothing less than the most rapid and radical expansion of their defences could give them any hope of preserving even a semblance of security on their northern frontiers. This expansion appears to entail an addition of at least Rs. 450-500 crores to defence expenditure. What will its impact be? Will it worsen existing strains? Will it retard the Plan? Or is it conceivable that its shock and discipline could help India to overcome the failures and bottlenecks which have so drastically held down its rate of growth?

The first consequence of extra spending on defence is likely to be increased purchasing power in the community. The new expenditure will be for defence goods, in other words, for goods which will not enter the market for sale and hence help to mop up the purchasing power made available by the salaries and wages earned in producing the defence goods. Unless this extra, unbalanced purchasing power is in some measure kept off the market, India risks inflation. I would remind you that prices are already on the rise, that the first two budgets of the Third Plan have already exceeded the "safe" limit of deficit financing—set at Rs. 100 crores a year, that food production cannot be very quickly expanded. True, new American releases of cotton and grain under Public Law 480 were announced at the end of 1962. But they cannot fill the whole potential gap. If the defence effort is not to be financed by inflation — which risks catastrophic pressures on food prices and is socially the most unjust and irresponsible way of going about the task — taxation and savings have to take up the slack.

In theory, there is still a margin for increased taxes and savings in India. Both are still under 10 per cent of national income and many economists argue that a government cannot really be held to be serious about development until 20 per cent of national income is secured for taxes. And a 15 per cent level of saving is often claimed to be the minimum compatible with "take off" into self-sustaining growth. The difficulty is, of course, the extreme poverty of India. Not to consume an important percentage of income would be the equivalent among many groups of slipping fatally below the level of subsistence. Taxes have in any case been going up. They were increased in both the most recent budgets — Rs. 85 crores in 1961/62, by Rs. 68.20 crores in 1962/63. The States, too, have increased their levies. The figure was Rs. 14 crores in 1961/62 and the new proposals for 1962/63 should bring in an extra Rs. 71 crores a year. Is there scope for more?

Middle class tax rates in India are rather lower than in Japan, agricultural incomes largely escape income tax, indirect taxes on such necessities as kerosene would help in the rationing process, business firms may benefit from the extra stimulus defence gives to the economy and could be expected to relinquish the extra profits, in spite of a 5 per cent increase in company taxation in the last budget. There are thus opportunities, but all of them present difficulties. More taxes on the poor could weaken national unity. More taxes on the middle class hit people most sorely beset by inflation. Business taxation can lessen essential capital formation. The choices before the Finance Minister, Morarji Desai, are not enviable. But a clear choice is better than the confused sacrifices and inequities of further inflation. His decision in the 1963/64 budget to raise Rs. 275 crores in further taxation is clearly correct.[1] But it does not cover the full sum of extra expenditure. Some purchasing power remains to be mopped up.

Could savings do more? The margin is there and the Finance Minister has called for an immediate increase in the savings rate from 8 to 15 per cent of national income. But, in fact, the habit of saving — as opposed to hoarding — has still to be learnt. Small savings consistently fell behind their target in the First and Second Plans and the response to patriotic appeals for higher saving since the emergency has been very uneven. By January 1962 the National Defence Fund had only received some Rs. 27 crores against expected receipts of Rs. 164 crores. Nor has there been much more success with the effort to tempt gold out of private hoards — where as much as Rs. 2,000 crores may be hidden away. In November 1962 Mr. Desai offered to buy gold at the international price ($35 an ounce) in return for 15-year bonds at the very attractive rate of 6½ per cent and

[1] One may, however, criticise some aspects of the taxation on business enterprise since, by hitting hardest firms which have accumulated large reserves for further development, it threatens to undermine India's greatest need—the need for growth.

free of the wealth and the capital gains tax. No questions would be asked, either, about the provenance of the gold. But by January 1963 subscriptions were still below Rs. 27 crores — Rs. 100 crores had been hoped for — and it remains to be seen whether the new measures making non-ornamental gold hoards illegal will encourage a greater flow. The truth probably is that the distrust of government and the fear of inflation which lead men to hoard in the first place have not been so dissipated by China's aggression as to modify the uncertainties and uneasiness of a lifetime.

One is left with the likelihood that not all the extra purchasing power can be mopped up by fiscal means. This possibility makes all the more urgent an effective and rapid physical mobilisation of resources.

At this point, I think one has to make one thing clear. There is no essential, total contradiction between the kind of mobilisation needed for an effective war effort and the kind of mobilisation which India needs to ensure the success of its Plan for development. In fact, I think one can safely say that quite a high percentage—we can guess and put it as high as 70 to 80 per cent — does not contradict the long-term aim of strengthening the Indian economy. The defence effort can speed up the development of power, the fulfilling of the steel target, a raising of the level of coal output, the turn-round of wagons and deliveries to factories and power plants. The expansion of certain forms of mechanical engineering, even though it takes place in ordnance factories, creates no insoluble problems of conversion against a happier day. Certainly the skills which are rapidly expanded in times of war for a bigger defence establishment are skills which are not lost. In fact, an expansion of the whole industrial working class can go forward; and, in the modern army, there is an added chance of a further dispersion of special skills. In short, the emergency, far from contradicting the Plan, could be an immense spur to its more rapid development. It is a fact that, again and again in human history, war efforts have been part of a decisive break-through to industrialisation, and there is no reason why, if the emergency is wisely handled, the same should not hold good for India.

With this possibility in mind, let us look at the various sectors and bottlenecks and try to assess the likely effect of the defence effort on them. I am not concerned at this point with the long-term difficulties—we will look at them later. Here it is just a question of the immediate impact and what can be done in the next twelve months.

To begin with a general point, it seems to me essential that the need for an effective centre of authority capable of deciding priorities should be urgently stressed. A cabinet of 50 members is not such a body. A lasting division of function between the Prime Minister's office, Finance, Defence, Economic Affairs and the Planning Commission could lead to prolonged confusion. This problem of decision plagues every country in time of emergency and one cannot say that any ideal solution has been worked out. But a small inner War Cabinet was found necessary in Britain, served by coordinating staff. There are special reasons in India for hoping that a greater concentration of decision-making will come about. Hitherto, Indian planning has seemed somewhat weak on the side of following-up speedily the decisions that are taken. Delays that are awkward in development become downright dangerous in defence. Clearer lines of responsibility could help to lessen the risk. Then the emergency demands closer coordination of the tasks of all the State governments. Sixteen separate governments reporting back to a body of 50 ministers hardly suggests speed and clarity. Above all, priorities cannot be weighed in a free-for-all between ministries. There must be some firm arbitration to decide not only on the priorities defence should enjoy but also on the points at which its claims should be overridden in the interest of other vital, supporting sectors. It is no use, for instance, permitting defence factories to engross so many extra scientists and engineers that transport or power development begins to falter.

To turn now to particular sectors, the impact of the emergency on agriculture may not, in direct terms, be very great—the amount of food that needs to be diverted from civilian consumption to an enlarged military establishment is relatively small. But the indirect effects could be great, either way. If farming is seriously down-graded in terms of essential capital, able administration, skilled staff and ministerial preoccupation, the emergency could worsen what is already a grave feature in agriculture — its relative failure, in spite of much rhetoric, to attract the men and the attention which really effective administration demand. We will come back to this point later. Here I only want to point out that preoccupation with the weapons and tools of a defence effort in camp and factory carries with it a certain unconscious down-grading of farm and field with possibly disastrous longer-term results.

There is, however, an opposite chance that the emergency can jerk the governments — at the Centre and in the States — into a new sense of opportunity on the land. Nothing, apparently, took India's leaders more by surprise than the response throughout India of ordinary men and women, the great majority of them country-dwellers, to the fact of aggression. Before the autumn of 1962, the picture given to outsiders of the state of the Indian Union seemed to be darkened on every side by communal divisions, linguistic differences and a growing break between North and South. In a trice, the Chinese abolished the feuds and set in their place a profound response to a sense of common Indian nationhood and destiny. I have myself seen in tiny villages in the hills of Gujarat, village headmen coming forward to press the savings of a lifetime into the collector's hand. The villagers gave in their jewellery, queued to be blood donors, besieged recruiting offices, all in an immense upsurge of a patriotism as profound as it was unforced.

This fact faces the Indian government with a risk and an opportunity. The risk is that, if a long indecisive period of "no-war, no-peace" ensues, the stimulus and fervour will die down but the bangles and the savings will have been irretrievably lost. The opportunity is to canalise the evident energies into works of rural construction which, in India, have been so often discussed and as often laid aside. A movement of National Defence Work, which could include the new Home Guards and village savings groups, might enable the government to get started all over India on such work as bunding, levelling, road-building and, above all, the completion of thousands of miles of minor irrigation channels. Some States have not yet passed the necessary legislation and the obstinacy of a single farmer can still prevent the final channels from being built. The central government has now sent out an urgent request for the legislation and a big effort on this front might permit India to finish by 1964 the 13 million acres of minor irrigation forecast in the Plan for 1965/66. Few policies could contribute so directly to that sharp rise in food output needed to counter the risks of inflation.

But one should, perhaps, enter a proviso here. The organising and sustaining of such a nation-wide effort—central backing, coordination with State governments, action by the Collectors, cooperation with Community Development officers would seem to require some innovations in leadership. Possibly an Office of Civilian Mobilisation working as the executive agent of the central ministries concerned would offer a possible solution.

Let us look now at the industrial side. The first point to underline is how much better equipped to deal with an emergency Indian industry has become as a result of ten years of uninterrupted growth and diversification. A glance at Table 2 will illustrate the range and variety of expansion that has taken place — the list has been chosen from categories essential to defence.

TABLE 2

INDUSTRIAL PRODUCTION FOR DEFENCE

	1950/51	*1955/56*	*1960/61*	*Capacity working %*
Machine tools (Rs. crores)	0.34	0.78	7.24	125
Copper ('000 tons)	6.6	7.5	8.8	118
Automobiles ('000 tons)	17.4	189.3	387	98
Steel ingots (mill. tons)	1.4	1.7	3.3	80-90
Steel castings & forgings ('000 tons)	—	15	69	80-90
Cement (mill. tons)	2.7	4.6	7.8	85
Finished steel (mill. tons)	0.98	1.3	3.3	75-80
Railway wagons (nos.)	2,924	8,393	13,826	50

Source: Indian Institute of Public Opinion.

If there are reserves that can be drawn into the industrial economic system, then the strain on the productive capacity of the economy is clearly less. One of the factors which undoubtedly helped mobilisation in Britain, and then again in

America, was the existence of unused industrial capacity and of trained unemployed industrial labour. In 1939, Britain still had a large pool of unemployed; it may, in fact, have been, at that time, the equivalent of 7 or 8 per cent of the labour force.

I think there is some possibility of setting unused capacity to work again here in India. One of the factors revealed in the foreign exchange crisis of the summer of 1962 was a disturbing amount of working at less than full capacity. In fact, in some industries probably not more than 60 per cent of the plant was being utilised. The collapse of the Stock Exchange in the autumn and the investors' extreme reserve also encouraged working at less than full capacity. And one should, I think, also mention a sort of psychological under-working, I mean, the slack which occurs when labour is disaffected and management discouraged.

I do not know whether one could put a quantitative estimate to all this. Table 2 attempts an estimate. In some key industries —machine tools, for instance—there is capacity working and two to three shifts. Some others reach 80 per cent. Very few fall as low as railway wagon production at 50 per cent. But the emergency does seem to have contributed at once to a lessening of the psychological difficulties. Everywhere there have been reports of workers offering no-strike pledges and asking to work overtime at normal rates. If management can canalise and maintain the enthusiasm, extra shift working and more output per man hour could, in theory, provide a large part of the needed extra production.

But this possibility depends in turn on the bottlenecks — coal, steel, power, transport, foreign exchange. How does the emergency affect them?

Once again, in theory, it could help. Industrial regulations have been modified to permit three shift working in the coal mines, at least for the time being. Under these conditions, the stagnation in coal output could end and the 97 million ton target for 1965/66 look a little less unrealistic. It is also thought that by the spring of 1963, all the new steel mills should be capable of operating at full capacity. This could bring crude steel output up from 4 million tons to the 6 million tons first forecast for 1960. But more steel and coal, to be effective, must be moved and here tighter management and more willing labour might cut some days off the turn-round of wagons. This in turn would enable coal to reach the power stations in a timely fashion—and since three-quarters of India's industry depends upon thermal stations, steady provision of power could immediately enhance production by cutting out the old uncertainties and shut-downs.

Nonetheless the amount of spare capacity that can be set to work does not depend wholly upon Indian efforts. One quickly comes up against the overwhelming problem — the shortage of foreign exchange. Although the extra steel is indigenous, though the extra coal is indigenous, the fact remains that the more a mine tries for accelerated coal production, the more it is up against the need for explosives and other maintenance materials which are still purchased from abroad. Although, virtually all consumer goods industries are having their allotments slashed, and the whole of the available foreign exchange is being diverted to essential sectors, I do not believe the diversions can fill the gap. One has to remember that in the summer of 1962 all import licences had already been halved and at least 80 per cent of India's imports are for essential goods in any case.

On what scale will the new demands for foreign exchange need to be financed? Nothing specific has been published so far. At present economic aid is running at the level of about a billion dollars a year. If we estimate that arms aid will come directly from military aid and defence support, then the sums needed for special steels and alloys, for petrol and wool and other vital supporting materials, might, at a guess, amount to another 200/300 million dollars a year.

The immediate position could, perhaps, be eased by transferring some existing aid from its link with future projects over to free exchange which can be spent rapidly on raw materials and maintenance imports. Yet the step is not easy. For instance, out of the 500 million dollars America makes available each year, over 100 million dollars are already provided in free exchange and, if one examines the composition of the rest of this sum, one finds that it is mainly earmarked for tools and machines which help in the further development of transportation and power. Nonetheless, in the immediate emergency, it might be possible to achieve some kind of switch from project aid for future factories to more aid for imports of spares and raw materials designed to maintain capacity production in already functioning factories.

Of course, the Western Powers might decide that this whole aspect of defence support should be dealt with on the basis of lend-lease, offshore purchases and all the other devices for burden-sharing which were worked out in the last war. I do not think the analogy irrelevant. In resisting crude aggression, India inevitably identifies its cause with the national freedom of the rest of the world. Holding the Chinese in check not only serves India's security but that of everybody else as well. Surely the lessons of past aggression are that every nation has a profound interest in seeing that those who want to use force do not get the idea that they can do so without fear or cost. India's security is in a real sense the security of its neighbours and friends as well.

I am not sure, however, whether this view of India's crisis is yet fully accepted. Until it is, the financing of extra military aid presents considerable difficulties. The American defence support programme for 1962 amounts, I believe, to about 1.6 billion dollars. The figure covers every part of the world and no one will be surprised to learn that there are a great many claimants for that support—some of them illegitimate, no doubt. Nonetheless, the pressures are there. India, with its new and utterly legitimate need to be supported against an unscrupulous aggressor, has to take its place in something of a queue. The issue is not simply that of putting India's claims at the top of the list. The sum itself available for defence support is not adequate to cover new claims. Recently, however, the Kennedy Administration, with immense persistence and hard work, has persuaded the Congress to accept a limited shift from direct defence support to economic aid. It is an ironic thought that one reason why the shift was made was because of the feeling that, within the non-aligned and neutral world, the change would be seen as a sign of good faith; now non-aligned India has rather different needs than seemed to be the case only a year ago. The American administration must in some measure reverse itself if it goes to the Congress to ask for more military support for India. And go it must for there are no spare funds.

What is likely to be the Western response to the need for an accelerated and sustained effort to help Indian defence? In point of fact, one cannot really assess what the internal strain and the pressure are going to be unless the scale of economic assistance from outside can be roughly assessed. Let us begin by saying that some of the supposed obstacles in the way of a greater Western effort are not obstacles at all. If you remember, there was a furore in the middle of 1962 over the question whether India would receive its billion dollars a year in Western aid if it insisted on buying MIGs from Russia. In the event, after a little frothing and fuming and some angry Senatorial comment, the year's allotment of economic assistance to India went forward smoothly. And I think the episode is a significant pointer to the way in which American and British policy has been moving in the last year.

The Kennedy Administration has been moving slowly and quietly for some time past — and especially since the Cuba crisis—towards a view long upheld by Mr. Macmillan. The position is that nothing must be done which intensifies the deterioration in relations between Russia and the West. The Cuban episode gave both sides the absolutely horrific picture of what it is like to be on the atomic brink. So the desire for a *détente* with Russia is higher in the West than ever before. In fact, we are now very nearly at the position where the West welcomes India buying MIGs to fight the Chinese as a symbol of the world ceasing to divide on purely ideological lines. The mood of seeing everything in terms of a tremendous Communist onslaught on the "free world" and the equal need to conduct an anti-Communist jehad has vanished away. The cool young men who now live in the White House are very uninterested in holy wars. What they want is a working relationship with Mr. Khruschev and to avoid the risk of world incineration. One may even say that to this extent America itself is now non-aligned. The suggestion that the West hesitates to give aid because India wants to go on being non-aligned is regarded with a sort of humorous fraternal indulgence. On the contrary, since non-alignment helps to prevent

Russia aligning itself automatically with China and keeps open the possibility of a Russo-Western *détente,* both London and Washington support non-alignment and are utterly opposed to the idea that India should spoil it by asking for formal military treaty relations with the West.

The Russian question is not decisive. I think that is clear. But there is another question which is infinitely more difficult for India and it, unhappily, is absolutely crucial. No friend of India should disguise the fact that the scale of assistance to India in the emergency will be greatly influenced by its relations with Pakistan. This does not spring from *parti pris*; it does not spring from favouring one side or the other; it does not even spring from any kind of judgment about the rights and wrongs of the Kashmir case, which seem to most people to be infinitely involved. It does spring from something quite different, yet absolutely basic — a shrewd military look at the northern frontier. Such a look inevitably instils the belief—which, I think, it would be hard to eradicate from the minds of Western chiefs-of-staff — that one cannot in the long run mount and maintain a credible defence against the Chinese on the northern frontiers if a strong, profound internal quarrel is continuing on this side of them.

There are a number of reasons for this belief, first and foremost the arguments of history. Nearly always a successful invasion has been able to exploit an internal struggle — by "internal" in this case, I mean on *this* side of the Himalayan barrier. I might remind you that the last time England was conquered—by the Normans—King Harold was away fighting the Scots; so what happened? England was taken over. If one wants to go a little further away, what happened to Montezuma? How was it that Cortez, almost unarmed, reached the court of the Aztecs? The answer is not in doubt. When Cortez landed, Montezuma was caught up in a fight between his tribes and the tribes on the coast. The coastal tribes simply took Cortez through the high passes, seeing in him the enemy of their enemy.

If one must include melancholy analogies which come nearer home. I doubt whether the British would have gained control of India if the Moghul Empire had not been at the point of collapse and the Marathas had not been busy fighting the Muslims. In fact, it is quite likely that the Marathas would have triumphed over the British had they not had their minds on other things. It is, in fact, the unanimous judgment of history that an internal struggle continuing at a time of external aggression fatally weakens the ability of any nation to withstand onslaught from outside.

Strategy tells the same story. The Ladakh front may not entail a fatal exposure of India's weakness. But in NEFA the blow could be lethal. Behind NEFA lies Assam, beyond and below Assam, access to India's essential industrial strength. Yet look at the map. Look at the frontiers of East Pakistan. Look at the Silliguri gap, only 30 miles wide and often flooded. Consider the possibility — *without* some kind of working understanding with Pakistan — of defending the eastern frontiers at all. The question of Pakistan is thus crucial to any long-term question of sustained defence, aimed at building up these frontiers so that the Indian experiment in peaceful economic growth can go forward uninterrupted by casual hammer blows from power-hungry neighbours.

India's friends outside cannot ignore these historical and strategic facts. They must in all honesty say that the outlook for effective defence is grim indeed without some kind of coordination with the Pakistanis and perhaps with the Burmese. The idea has, in fact, been put forward by such distinguished Indian leaders as Mr. K. M. Pannikar. He has written of the possibility of a defence community designed to safeguard the integrity of the whole northern frontier.

I know that some Indians tend at this point to protest that after Pakistan's recent readiness to work with the Chinese, no cooperation is possible. Yet the reaction of the Pakistanis to the Chinese aggression, though regrettable, illustrates precisely the point India's friends are trying to make — that if a nation tolerates an agonising, embittered and venomous quarrel inside its frontier, an external aggressor need not confine himself to direct pressure. He can play one side off against the other. The emotional levers are put into his hands. He can play upon the temper, the violence, the distrust of the disputants just as contemptuously as Rosencranz and Guildenstein tried to play on

Hamlet's emotions. In other words, the aggressors treat the quarrellers as malleable instruments, as emotional raw material for their own plans. The fact that the Pakistanis have reacted in precisely this way makes it, in one sense, much more difficult to reach a settlement. But in another it only underlines with increased intensity the urgent need to see that a settlement is reached.

Successful negotiation of an envenomed issue means compromise and "give and take," and a number of compromises are, of course, under discussion. What any outsider thinks about the possible compromises is wholly unimportant; the issue is to find one acceptable to the parties concerned. But it may be helpful to outline one or two that are under discussion now. One lies in a fairly drastic reorganisation of the cease-fire line, which would give the Pakistanis some of the upper waters of the Chenab and a larger part of the upper Indus valley. This, I believe, India might have negotiated two years ago. I question whether Pakistan would accept it now; still, it is one of the possibilities. Secondly, there is the possibility of trying to get a West Irian type of solution. The disputed area, in this case the Valley of Kashmir, is put under U.N. Trusteeship, with the eventual choice of independence. This would have the advantage that it does, as it were, withdraw the centre of the dispute from the claim of rival sovereignty. Another possibility would lie in trying to do in Kashmir what the French and the Germans achieved in a sense in the Saar. One does not solve the problem in terms of itself, but one changes the context within which an ultimate reconciliation can take place. In other words, if over the next 10 to 15 years, the Indians and the Pakistanis determine to form a defence community and an economic community with an increasing degree of economic mobility and interdependence, the outcome might be an environment into which an autonomous Kashmir might fit — as a sort of Asian Andorra. I would not mention some of the more frivolous suggestions, such as that the Swiss should be given Kashmir and the foreign exchange earned by tourism as a result should be divided on a per capita basis between the two countries.

But, perfectly seriously, the only way in which a compromise solution is likely to be found over Kashmir is for both Indians and Pakistanis to come to feel profoundly that the threat beyond the northern frontier is greater than any of their internal differences, that this running sore is now profoundly affecting their ability to survive as independent countries and that the highest priority of all has to be given to finding a solution for this ultimately fratricidal struggle *within* the northern frontier.

It is difficult at this stage for India's friends in the West to know quite how to handle this problem. If they say, "Well, long-term assistance to be effective must depend upon a settlement," they look like blackmailers trying to force out of India when it is weak the concessions it would not make when it was strong. The question whether the nation was sensible when it was strong is not raised at this point. On the other hand, Indians have to try to realise the implications of the fact that the question of defence support to India has got to go back to Congress and to Parliament, that very substantial sums of other people's tax money are at stake, that the arguments for added assistance have to sound reasonably convincing to a large and not always well-informed electorate. There is some difficulty in arguing for generous and effective long-term defence support so long as the dispute with Pakistan creates such vulnerability along the Himalayas and allows critics of ill will to suggest that the arms could be used against Pakistan. This is not a question of taking sides. It is a problem of finding convincing arguments to persuade elderly Congressmen and harassed Conservative M.P.s that their electors will think it reasonable to be taxed for such an uncertain venture.

This is the fundamental political problem. Let me repeat. Soviet Russia's support of India presents no difficulty to the West. I am sure that the West would be absolutely delighted if Mr. Khruschev's dispatch of MIGs to India meant that Mr. Khruschev had some more rude words to call "the Albanians." But the issue of Pakistan confronts the Western world with profound dilemmas of political and parliamentary persuasion and as such it cannot just be wished away or brushed aside or dismissed. It could affect the whole nature of India's defence relationships. It could affect the whole tempo at which outside assistance flows in — or does not flow in — to meet India's intensified needs. And since, in the long run as well as the short, access to foreign exchange remains one of the chief keys both to India's defence and to its development plans, the question-mark over Indian-Pakistani relations is a question-mark over the country's whole prospects of effective survival and growth.

2

Planning for Growth

THE immediate emergency, thrust upon India by Chinese aggression, has underlined two major difficulties. The first is the disappointing performance of a number of key sectors in the economy — in other words, the economy's slow rate of growth. The second is the biting shortage of foreign exchange which places further curbs on expansion. The emergency has underlined them. But they were there before it and could outlast it unless the extra urgency and energy it breeds can lead both India and India's friends abroad to take a fresh look at the difficulties.

The First Plan ended in 1956 in an atmosphere of some euphoria. By setting under-used, war-developed capacity to work fully and by completing schemes started soon after independence, industry achieved a very favourable capital-output ratio.[1] The weather was kind and gave such bumper harvests in 1953/54 that many people erroneously attributed the rise in output to irrigation, better methods and the success of Community Development. Above all, foreign exchange faced little or no stringency. India's sterling balances were not exhausted and all its primary exports earned record returns in the post-Korean boom.

The spectre of slow growth and low reserves began to appear in 1957 and, since that time, the Indian economy, in spite of steady growth, has always run behind its targets. Perhaps the simplest fashion of illustrating the shortfall is once again through a table: (Table 3). Similarly in the first two years of the Third Plan, output has been disappointing. As I have already pointed out, nearly all the indices for agricultural production in 1961/62 were static or falling and industry's rate of advance has been held back as a result.

[1] Such a ratio is very favourable if each unit of fresh capital achieves a unit of added output. A more normal ratio is 3 of capital to 1 of output.

TABLE 3
SOME SECOND PLAN RESULTS

	Target 1956-1961	*Actual achievement*	*Difference %*
	(Rs. Millions at 1952-53 prices)		
Plan outlay	48	41	— 18
Investment	62	60	— 3
Savings	52	41	— 20
Money Supply	36	29	
External Payments Deficit	10	21	+107
Food Imports	2.4	7.9	+240
Estimated foreign assistance*	8	15	+ 84
Withdrawal of Reserves*	2	6	+200
	Growth rate 1956/61 per cent		
National Income	25	18-19	— 24
Industrial output	64	42	— 34
Mining	50	22	— 56
Agriculture	18	19	+ 5

* At current prices. *Source: The Economist Intelligence Unit.*

In all this, one factor of growth has, however, surpassed all expectations. The Second Plan had estimated that in 1961 India's population would have grown to 408 millions. In fact, it reached 438 millions — an annual rate of increase of 2 per cent. With growth in national income not exceeding 3.5 per cent, the margins for rising consumption and investment were thus exceedingly narrow.

At this early point I feel, therefore, that something should be said about the problems posed by the pressure of growing population on India's still-limited resources. I must confess that I personally feel a certain modesty in coming and lecturing other people on the issue of what they should do about their population. I know that it is an immensely popular pursuit among many distinguished Western leaders and I respect their sense of purpose and dedication. Yet I feel that this is a subject on which countries must take their own decisions without too much exhortation from outside. In other words, there will be no long lecture from me on the necessity of having fewer Indians.

There is, however, one issue I wish to raise. Over and over again one encounters the belief—often stated with the dogmatism of a proven fact—that without population control there can be no economic growth. It is not unknown in the Western world to hear the statement that it is absolutely no use helping a country whose population is still increasing at the rate prevailing in India. Now, this I believe to be a radical misconception. Far from a slower rate of growth in population determining economic growth, economic growth determines the trend towards smaller families. It is economic development, in fact, that gives people the incentives to want smaller families. I assume we are not yet postulating a World Population Council which will say: "Now, Mrs. Smith, you have 2.3 children and this is .3 too many; what are you going to do about it?" We are thinking, I take it, in terms of what parents actually want. It is really only when economic growth begins in earnest that enough parents see it to be in the profound interest of their family, their own children and, indirectly, of their community to bring up only that size of family which they can provide with food, health, education and reasonable opportunity.

This has, in fact, proved the pattern of population in cultures as different as those of Western Europe and of Japan. The last two hundred years have proved that when people *want*, for a whole variety of economic and social reasons, to have smaller families, they do, in fact, have smaller families. The number of children begins to diminish when the inducements to concentrate upon the well-being of children begin to increase—when child labour comes to an end, and reliable children are no longer the greatest single asset of old age, when epidemics are brought under control, and parents no longer feel they have to produce twelve children if they hope to raise three, when skilled and educated labour, not numbers and brawn, begin to determine the labour market. The trend can be observed in Japan; it can be observed in Western Europe; in fact, the only country where the trend has been once more reversed back towards greater numbers is in the affluent United States: I wonder whether the time will come for some very serious-minded Indian delegations to go to America and preach the doctrine of fewer Americans?

Given the historical evidence we have, it is wrong and, indeed, dangerous, to suggest that economic development and economic aid given to that development must depend upon a reduction in the birth-rate. It is an especially inappropriate connection at a time when, as in India, increasing population is partly due to the lengthening of life. The only known way of lowering the birth-rate is to hasten the processes of economic growth and the assistance which accelerates them. This does not mean that aid-givers may not stress the degree to which population pressure nullifies growth. It does not mean that every effort should not be made through better research to find acceptable means of controlling fertility. But what is inadmissible is the remark so often made in the West: "Well, you cannot help those people because they have so many children." If one had used this argument about Japan 80 years ago, one would have foreseen continued stagnation. Yet Japan now is a classic example of a population which, after reaching the highest rates of growth, reverted towards stability.

It is, in fact, sobering to remember that 80 years ago the Malthusian argument that the poor always bred too fast was used to counter all the early efforts at social welfare. Both the case of Japan and of working-class Europe reinforces the point. When the process of economic growth, social change, and, I would add, the education of women, go forward, families fall to the level at which parents can raise them with reasonable elbow room—which, surely, is the fundamental meaning of parental responsibility. There will, no doubt, continue to be a vital moral debate about the means of birth control but there can be surely no debate over the injustice and cruelty of bringing into the world children who will be barely able to eat, who will be crippled with disease and after a brief life of pain and deprivation will be snuffed out before they reach their teens. The profound miseries of millions of the world's children will end only when economic development has been successfully pushed forward with every possible means of economic assistance from the outside world and by every possible means of internal economic mobilisation.

Let us turn now to the problems raised by India's relative slow rate of economic growth. We can usefully start where the outlines of the future Indian economy are being shaped—in the planning process itself. Let me say straight away that anything I may advance on the difficulties and delays that have been encountered must be put in the context of the overwhelming, the really titanic scale of the tasks which planners and administrators have to face. No government has ever before tried to administer with freedom and decentralized authority a nation of 450 million people, dispersed in sixteen states and speaking half a dozen major languages. To achieve civic order and legal government is in itself a formidable achievement—one, certainly, that has escaped Latin America with one-half as many people and one-third of the languages. To administer in addition a dynamic economy planned for welfare and development implies a range of responsibilities of an even more taxing kind. The most totally literate and educationally advanced community would find the task formidable. Given the size of India's educated cadre at Independence—about 400,000 students graduating each year in a population of nearly 400 million—and given the fact that British rule was "law-and-order" rule, only indirectly related to welfare and wholly unrelated to economic growth, then one has to admit that the achievement is the vital thing, not the shortcomings which have sometimes seemed to overshadow it.

However, it is by facing the weaknesses that even better results can be secured. Let us look at the planning process itself. In many ways it has steadily improved. The First Plan was little more than an assemblage of desirable projects, some of them already launched. It was not until the Second Plan that a real attempt at forecasting was made—with the facts on national income, on saving, on industrial and agricultural possibilities and performance assembled in an orderly way. The background to the Third Plan again demonstrates greater sophistication—more detailed in-put, out-put analysis, more specific calculation of future needs, clearer efforts to see that the various sectoral plans complement each other and make up a coherent whole. Indeed, it can be said that Indian planning has become the model of planning all round the world in all mixed, developing economies. Yet the rate of growth still lags. Why?

I would like to underline what I believe to be two of the

major difficulties. The first concerns administration, the second, technique or approach. I think it is not unfair to say that from the beginning Indian planning has been stronger on formulation than on implementation—or, less pompously put, on thinking things out rather than getting things done. The bias springs in part from inheritance. Delhi was moulded on the Whitehall model and, as Britain discovered between 1945 and 1950, men trained in the tradition of equity and precedent do not always take kindly to the short-cuts and quick decisions of an effective follow-up. For a long time there seemed to be no specific point in the structure of government at which active and, if necessary, angry officials asked why decisions reached months ago had not been put into effect. It was in military parlance as though there were Q plans, but no Q ops.

In the last few years, the Planning Commission itself, with its evaluation teams and its contacts with the State governments, has attempted to fill the gap. But the degree to which one government department can effectively prod another is limited—and the Planning Commission has tended to grow into one. This issue is so urgent, the risk of delay so great, the loss of development through loss of time so dangerous that one wonders whether a sub-committee of the cabinet or some other high-level body reporting directly to the Prime Minister should not undertake the responsibility of seeing, month by month, that planned development is going forward at a coherent pace and that the various schemes and sectors hang together. *Could* the bottlenecks in basic industries have developed so far if a strong cabinet body had been breathing down the neck of the Minister responsible for coal mines and demanding why, month after month, his figures were below target?

Possibly the emergency will help here. If a small War Cabinet or committee of the cabinet oversees the rapid expansion of the defence effort it could acquire the taste for results as well as programmes. Then it would have the experience needed to ensure, after the emergency, that urgency and speed do not fade from the direction of the economy.

A speedy and effective checking on performance would be needed in any system of planning. But in India's mixed economy where Delhi's oversight over the whole system makes every sector, public or private, subject to the decisions that are taken at the Centre, the need for speedier decisions and greater concentration on action and results is overwhelming. Over a whole range of issues, effective administration may demand the abandonment of direct controls. Once the emergency is passed, it is arguable that enterprises, private and public, should be left to struggle for themselves to secure cement and steel and power and building sites. There would be inequities, no doubt, and some wrong decisions. But they cannot equal in devastating effect the infinite delays of referring priorities to Delhi, there to be worked out by officials who, all too often, have no more sense of priority than the man requesting the licence. They may, in fact, have less. He at least has a vital interest—to make a profit and keep in business, whether he is the director of Hindustan Machine Tools in the public sector or head of a private steel works. But the official in Delhi has chiefly to avoid making a mistake. This is not a spur to decision-making. Delay—which may be the greatest mistake of all—will not appear as a blot on his record.

True, the limiting case of intensely scarce foreign exchange cannot be dismissed. Some licensing has to continue. But it is surely not necessary—as has been the practice hitherto—to license each particular element in an allocation as well as the allocation itself. Is there not a case, too, for forming industrial groups and giving them a block issue of foreign exchange to work out between them? No doubt, some firms may profit unduly. But is that more damaging than that delay should prevent them all from making a profit and hence cut back their possibilities of further investment?

Now I would like to turn to another factor in planning. It is not enough in estimating future needs to establish the physical components of what is to be produced—to make sure that there is enough steel for the railways, coal for the power stations and power for everything. These physical availabilities are immensely important and some of them—transport and power above all—condition everything else. But combining them in such a way as to achieve maximum growth involves more than physical calculations. The combination must release the greatest amount of resources for further investment. Otherwise, a great deal of physical resources can be used up and actually produce *dis-investment*—the absorption of precious materials into undertakings which earn no surplus themselves, yet deprive enterprises that might have done so from starting up.

So a calculation of the cost of projects and of the likely release of further resources that can be looked for as a result of incurring the cost is an essential part of planning. The profitability of an undertaking is more vital to growth than even a correct calculation of the materials going into it. To take an extreme case, the amount of bricks and mortar going into a museum or a powerhouse may be equivalent. The difference in their immediate earning power decides which of them a poor community ought to aim to have first.

All this I know is very obvious but it is surprising how often, in the planning process, cost—and profit—consciousness seem to be lacking. Let me give you some instances of what I mean. Because there is a certain prejudice against the idea of capitalists making a lot of money, it is often thought that the rate of return on capital ought to be low. But interest is the *price* of capital and if you put the price low, it is the equivalent, for planning, of saying that capital is cheap. But capital is, on the contrary, the scarcest commodity in any poor, developing country, and, since it is scarce and precious, it should be dear. If the price—interest—is kept too low, this scarce, indispensable resource will be used carelessly. It will go into enterprises giving little return. It will not be available for enterprises that could have brought in much more. Since the early stages of development do entail large expenditures on projects with very little prospect of quick direct returns—schools, health centres, urban housing—it is all the more vital that planning should concentrate in other fields on the projects which earn high rates and turn the capital over in the shortest space of time.

In fact, one should allow interest rates to rise sharply—one can always tax the bankers—in order to reflect capital's scarcity and the planners might well adopt as an essential yardstick the rule that, save in exceptional circumstances, the green light should be given only to enterprises that earn ten per cent on their capital and amortise themselves in a decade. With such a rule, a plan will not end up with too many high dams earning 2 per cent over 80 years, too many factories designed for making factories, too many public buildings earning almost nothing, too many public services—again power and transport—charging less than the going rate to cover interest and obsolescence on the grounds that, as public services, they should be run at cost. It has always seemed to me that much of the success in Japan's early planning was due to the degree to which the planners concentrated on agricultural productivity and on small industry with high returns. The larger enterprises—steel, armaments, machine-building—were introduced more slowly. It is in Russia, with its vast supplies of coal and iron ore, that heavy industry received such an overriding priority. It may be that the Japanese pattern is sounder.

So far, it does not seem to have attracted as much attention. The planners' temptation is always to leave the big things in the Plan. The political leaders like them. They have a prestige value. Often they are in the public sector. In any case, if during a plan period, something has to be abandoned, it is difficult to cut the big projects. Half a dam is not just half as efficient. It contributes nothing. So the cuts always land on the little projects further down the list—the medium irrigation, the local tannery, the extra industrial estate. Yet it is precisely the multiplicity of smaller enterprises, using little capital and earning good returns, that provides the profits and hence the capital for the next phase of advance.

It is just because the vital role of profits—in the public as in the private sector—has been neglected in the world's various "socialistic patterns" that growth has often been slow—as in parts of Eastern Europe—or living standards have remained so relatively low—as in the Soviet Union. Why is Mr. Khruschev now turning to the idea of "the firm" as a basic economic unit and urging that the firm be profitable? It is because the statistics of Russia's *physical* expansion have disguised appalling waste and misuse of resources. Steel output can go up and up but if the factories into which it goes produce shoes with two left feet or coats which the Soviet consumer now refuses to buy, the physical statistics are misleading. They suggest genuine growth and hence rising standards. But a bad shoe is not a productive fact. It is waste and you cannot improve the economy's performance or the peoples' living standards by accepting waste. So Mr. Khruschev is feeling his way back to the stern discipline of profits. Only thus can the genuine contribution of factories to real growth be measured--whether they are state enterprises or private firms.

The risk to effective planning of accepting wrong yardsticks of real cost can be illustrated in another way. Twice Indian estimates of needed foreign exchange have proved to be grievously wrong—in 1957/58 and again in 1962/63. Two years after the beginning of each Plan period, it is discovered that far more foreign exchange is being absorbed than was estimated in the Plan itself. Some factors we will discuss later—the weakness in world primary prices, the tendency of imported manufactures to rise in price, the lack of "free exchange" in the available aid. But here I want to suggest that the rupee is almost certainly overvalued and in calculating their need for imports, public and private managers may well be encouraged to treat imports as "cheap" and to neglect the strenuous search for and development of indigenous resources. If I may illustrate this point from my own experience, I recently visited a mill; it was the latest thing; it had just been built with all the latest technologies from Japan; the gleaming, electronic looms stretched on and on; it was going to give work to all of thirty people. So I said: "Will this fine mill produce for the export market?" They said: "A little, yes, but mainly for the domestic market." Then I said: "How about the raw materials?" "Oh! they are all imported," they said, "India has no indigenous pulp industry at present." Yet, the day before, I had been taken up into the mountainous, forested part of the State, and heard officials complain about the difficulty of providing extra income for their forest-dwelling tribals. In the forests, no pulp industry; at the port, a plant costing crores, giving virtually no fresh employment, serving only the domestic market and relying on imports of pulp for its raw materials. It would be hard to picture a more complete contradiction of India's true needs and I doubt whether such a perversion of true planning could have occurred in an economy in which foreign exchange was valued—as it should be—"above rubies."

I do not suggest that the answer is devaluation. India's opportunities of increasing its exports are so meagre that I cannot believe it would benefit from a cut in their earning capacity. But might not an "accounting price" be fixed in the planning process which would give the rupee a truer exchange value? In other words, in making the estimates, could not all imports be calculated as costing more? And might not a tax on import licences, or possibly the auctioning of import licences, compel the industrialist to use his imports more carefully? Once again, I know that distrust of business people and fear that a few big firms would engross all the licences makes the government reject the idea of auctioning and it is true that the import duties introduced in the 1963 budget may help in this respect. But will they go far enough? Might auctioning supplement their effect? Business men do not bid for licences they cannot use profitably and the more profitably they are used, the more capital accumulates for further investment. The government can tax distributed profits more heavily. It can increase, if need be, expenditure taxes and duties on luxury goods—although, once again, the new budget leaves little margin—but do not prevent the profits being made in the first place. This should be the first law of a developing economy—yet the latest budget seems once again to underestimate this fact.

I would like now to try to trace these two difficulties—administrative and managerial shortcomings and inattention to profitability—through the agricultural and industrial sectors. Once again, let me repeat my sense of the right context for these remarks. To bring change, radical change, to 500,000 villages cannot be done overnight. Nor can it be accomplished without a vast increase in the number of competent technicians modernised agriculture demands. To achieve a 40 per cent increase in food output over the last 12 years is a very considerable achievement, especially when we remember that this growth follows decades of stagnation and even regression. Nevertheless, I think that agriculture is handicapped by administrative shortcomings and by some lack of appreciation of the profit motive or, if you like, of incentives. In fact, I believe that many of the particular problems can be only understood in the light of these two wider issues.

Most of the theoretical solutions to low agricultural productivity are now well known. They have been known for ten years. Irrigation, the right fertiliser, improved seed, better cultivation and better implements can double and treble output. Better storage can prevent the loss of 10 to 15 per cent of the crop. Adequate credit can break the peasants' dependence on the usurer—who is still said to provide 80 per cent of India's rural lending. Cooperatives take the peasant out of reach of the middlemen. Roads bring him to market. There is no secret about this essential core of any effective programme of agricultural reform. The trouble lies in its patchy implementation and, if any one reason more than any other lies behind the patchiness, it is the lack of administrative concentration and skill. On the technical side, I doubt very much whether the universities are producing enough young agronomists—agriculture was the only school to experience a fall in graduates between 1950 and 1956. I doubt whether they are being sufficiently persuaded to work actually in the countryside. Village level workers often know no more than the farmers, who do not respect someone who cannot in fact advise. The block officer may know more but his availability is restricted by the number of villages he has to cover and his difficulties with transport.

On the side of administration proper, from the highest level downwards, agriculture gets priority in rhetoric but rarely in fact. No Chief Minister in a State has taken over the portfolio of agriculture. The bright entrants to the civil service head for the old levers of power—finance—or for the new prestige areas like industry. No young collector is likely to feel that his promotion will depend absolutely on raising productivity per acre in his district. The urgency and interest are simply not there. So the known solutions do not receive that charge of administrative drive and follow-through which would help them to get off the ground.

This phenomenon, I may say, can be seen in agriculture all round the world. The Cinderella of the colonial services, it has entered Independence in a depressed state and has not yet recovered. The better methods may be known but the men to carry them out are lacking. The result is all too often a tolerant acceptance in agriculture of slacknesses and inefficiencies which on the railways, in public works, in industry would lead to courts of enquiry.

Let me illustrate more concretely what I mean. All through India and Pakistan, you will encounter the phenomenon of dams that are finished and feeder channels that are not. When the corps of engineers or the contractor who is going to build a dam sets to work, what happens? They put the on-site roads in first; if cement is lying about before the monsoon, they cover it because otherwise they know it will be useless. In any case, they have seen to it that it has arrived on time. A trained labour force has been assembled, or at least within the limits set by the desperate shortage of skills. Housing has been provided for the workers. In other words, the project has been prepared and laid out in a systematic way.

When we turn to the village, there is little of this orderly procedure. The channels have not been dug because Mohan Lal refuses his permission. The "on-site" roads may be built but, just as regularly as clock-work, they are cut off for three months during the monsoon. The degree to which the fertiliser does not arrive before the harvest has become a sort of wry joke from one end of the country to the other. When it does, it lies about in rotting sacks and coagulates. Improved seed farms are allowed to run down and, when the seed appears, it is found to be very unimproved. One could continue the list. The sort of disproportion between the aims of policy and what is actually done would not occur if farming were approached with the professional competence apparent in, say, building dams. And I cannot help thinking, the lack of professionalism is due to the low actual priority suffered by agriculture both in technical recruitment and political interest. If a "project area" were approached in the spirit of a big public works project—with the same business and professional skills—I believe India's food problems could be solved in short order.

Nor can one use the alibi that the farmers resist change. In many districts this is no longer true. They are positively harrying the officials to get more support and better results. The farmer is often ready to pay black market prices for fertiliser if he can get his hands on it; he is prepared to put up the work and money for the local road, if somebody will come and give it a tarmac top. In area after area, local energy is not lacking. What *is* lacking is the effective entrepreneurial, professional and administrative background into which this local enterprise can fit.

I believe, too, that greater emphasis on making farming pay would also accelerate necessary changes. Building up the farmers' income has negative aspects—ending his dependence on the *bania* and the middleman. It has positive aspects—enlarging by at least a third the flow of credit to the farmer, moving seriously to give him support prices, which make extra work and fertiliser worth while. Perhaps, too, many people have seen Community Development not as a way in which the farmer can be helped to make money but, rather, as a way to persuade him to lead a purer, better life. Now, I am all for the farmer doing it, though I suspect *he* will decide whether he will or not. But of one thing I am sure. He needs a larger income if he is to enjoy any of the possibilities of a larger life.

Once again, a concrete illustration may better illustrate my meaning. One of the most lively centres of village expansion I have encountered is to be found at Anand in Gujarat. The starting point was the link between a first-class dairy under highly skilled direction, the large milk market of Bombay and the farmers of Kaira District with their buffaloes. By making the dairy the core of a cooperative and collecting the milk daily from the farmers for cash payment, the scheme has drawn the whole district into a creative and stimulating relationship with the market.

As a result of this experience, the farmer has acquired more than a better income; he is beginning to ask the right things about what he should do with his income. Today, for instance, he says: "Wouldn't I be much better off if my cow gave twice as much milk?" Now, you can spend ten years telling him this —rushing in on a motor-bicycle and saying: "What you need is a better cow," and rushing out again—but the farmer will do nothing about it. It is only when he has in fact been assured of a steady market for his milk, and thus the incentive to produce it, that the blinding insight strikes him—with a better cow he could do twice as well.

What does he do at this point? Being a shrewd man, he decides to put some of the cooperative's earnings into an artificial insemination centre and into a cattle-feed factory. Incidentally, on the side, he puts in a lime-crushing plant too to provide a little subsidiary income and keep his limes from glutting the urban market. In other words, out of the right kind of structure flow the right kind of inducements to the farmer and the right kind of growth. His increased capital inputs have been earned already by his ability to make a profit on his milk. The original base of the operation—the daily collection of milk from a score of villages by a milk cooperative in whose profit they share—may seem small. But, launched on the right lines, the nucleus creates further growth. Today, Anand is a big profitable enterprise with half a crore of annual turnover and it is providing its own capital for further expansion. Surely it is a most striking example of what market incentives, properly used, can achieve.

I wonder, too, whether this realistic, and, if you like, hard-headed approach to agriculture might not help in one of India's unique obstacles to rising productivity—I mean, the problem of the cow. Now I must repeat an earlier remark. The last thing I wish to do is to lecture people about their cultural patterns. I mention this problem simply because it is vital to the farming revolution India needs and because so many Indians have said: "The cow slaughter that we have—which is to leave animals to die of starvation—is the most cruel kind of cow slaughter imaginable. Cannot something be done about it?" What I would like to suggest is that something can be done within the context of what the farmer has an economic interest in doing.

One of the possibilities lies in the building of modern abattoirs where the beasts can be painlessly slaughtered and the by-products used. Yet, for sensitive people, this method is perhaps too perilously close to direct cow slaughter. Another possibility has therefore been put forward—the building of desiccating plants for fallen animals. A desiccating plant tries to use what is usable in the hide and in the carcase of the cow, for exports of hides and for bone-meal and fertiliser. This method does not take up any direct position on the issue of cow slaughter. It simply tries to avoid waste once the animal is dead. The farmer is thus offered an incentive to think about alternatives to simply allowing the animals to starve.

There are perhaps 80 million surplus cows in a country very near the limit even for human feeding. The choice between better, healthier children and the continuance of useless cows is hardly one that can be evaded. In one sense, perhaps, the problem of the cow is not unique to India. In Africa where cows are still reckoned not as an investment but as a status symbol, or as a bride price, there is a cultural problem to be resolved. Of course, since it *is* a cultural problem, many devout and sincere Indians will make nothing of the economic argument. If it is sinful to kill a cow, no amount of explanation about the value of hides for export will make any difference. We do not kill our grandparents for their gold teeth. But I feel perhaps justified in mentioning the issue, not simply because of its immense economic significance, but because the cultural argument itself seems faulty. From what one gathers in rural areas, the cows do appear to get the very worst of the bargain—dying in a slow misery of starvation—and this surely is a very odd outcome for a doctrine which was clearly designed to ensure the loving care and up-keep of the cow. There is here a certain disproportion which perhaps an outsider may mention without appearing to intervene gratuitously and discourteously in other people's cultural patterns. Nor from an economic point of view can it be denied that the load useless cows represent upon the Indian economy is almost insupportable.

There is one further point I would like to make before we move on to industrial questions. I believe a clearer view on profitability might encourage an approach to agriculture more clearly based on the concept of the *best* use of land. Self-sufficiency in food can certainly be attained since Indian yields are still so low and the gap is relatively small. But self-sufficiency is not a final answer. If much of Indian land can earn more through cotton, groundnuts, spices, fruit, soya or any other commercial crop, it is certainly not against the interests of the economy to use the sales of commercial crops to buy food abroad. The important point is optimum land use and this implies a concept of profitability. It is only when agriculture is seen as a flexible, varied, expendable source of all manner of supplies—industrial supplies fully as much as food supplies—

that it can play its full role in Indian development. Indeed, harking back for one moment to my example of the rayon mill, I would like to suggest the country's interest in seeing the land play its full part as an *industrial* provider. It may be that the spectre of a foreign exchange shortage which keeps factories working at 40 per cent below capacity cannot be wholly exercised in orthodox terms of increasing exports. We will look at this possibility later on. But if it is the case, then indigenous industrial supplies become infinitely more important.

If I may make a digression, I would like, at this point, to mention a small obsession—the role of wood in developing economies. The rayon mill's lack of pulp is a good instance. Now that wood can be treated against ants, it could be a much more widely used and attractive building material. It has an essential protective part to play. When I was over in the Damodar Valley recently—after an absence of ten years—I could see that the organisation of the dams, of irrigation, of flood control, had all gone ahead dramatically. The Valley has become one of the great industrial power-houses of the country. Industry is developing on every side, above all the big steel giants at Burnpur and Durgapur. Yet, during the visit, one official echoed the concern I had heard expressed in 1952. "You know," he said, "it is very worrying; we still really haven't got on to the conservation problem in the water-sheds;" and one or two of the experts said: "If we are not careful and quick, these dams will have silted up in 30 years." In other words, just for the planting of a few trees, one risks losing the whole power complex based upon the dams. Why is the connection not made? I will tell you. Because trees have no glamour. Dams have glamour; steel has glamour; but, when it comes to the honest little aspen that you plant up in the water-shed, nobody behaves as though it were worth thinking about. Yet, good afforestation is within the reach of any developing economy. It must in some way be given glamour. I do not mean a great tamasha during which, on one day a year, everyone plants a tree—for the goats to eat. I mean a full-scale, nation-wide drive for re-afforestation. I mean a Ministry of Forestry. I mean trees as an essential part of community development and respect for trees as part of rural education. Why not train the little boys to control the goats? Why not, as in Cyprus, plant fruit trees between villages and plantations so that the villagers, not wishing to lose the fruit, keep the goats tethered?

Once the sense of the trees' vital importance grows in the countryside, one can think of further vital contributions. Given the expense of electrification on a nation-wide basis, I, for one, doubt whether village electricity is likely to be possible in this country. Why not try the experiment made in some parts of Africa—that of basing a village generator on a small village plantation, on a sustained yield basis and perhaps reinforced by solar energy? Too much of our thinking about development is conditioned by the experience of Russia and North America —continents with such vast supplies of coal and iron ore that massive thermal electrification and a quick advance to the heaviest of heavy industry made perfect economic sense. But India resembles the other developing continents—Africa, Latin America—in being comparatively short of major supplies of energy and lacking a whole range of essential minerals. May it not be a more sensible pattern of growth to look to the land for a great mass of renewable materials and to attempt a more decentralised, small-scale Japanese type of advance? Today, when interruptions to the regular supply of raw materials has become a major factor in India's slow rate of growth, when factories working below capacity are in some measure the chief symbol of what has gone wrong, it may be that a fresh look at the whole pattern of industrialisation needs to be given and a quite new priority and urgency given to the possibilities of wood and oilseeds and cotton and fibres.

Such a reconsideration might incidentally help more directly in India's daunting problem of unemployment. Like the rayon mill, the heaviest forms of industry swallow down capital and provide only marginal new employment. A £12 million refinery employs 350 people. The early Japanese pattern of artisans, cottage industries and small enterprise—more like a Milky Way than five or six large planets—may be a better model at this stage.

Thus insensibly we have moved from agriculture to industry —and this is right, since in fact they are the Janus heads of a single productive process, indispensable to each other, each determining what the other can effectively do. So now let us look at the twin problems of administration and profitability in the industrial sector.

It seems to me that Indian planning began, not unnaturally, with many of the moods and reactions of British opinion after the war. There was the same desire to make a fresh start, the same sense that, after the collapse of the thirties, the market could not be relied on, the same widespread hunger for "fair shares"—indeed, a much deeper hunger in India where the extremes of wealth and poverty are so much greater; a considerable confidence—after the experience of a war economy—in government as a stimulator and director and, among many people, an equal lack of confidence in business decisions and business motives. A rawer, rougher, newer industrial leadership in India made the suspicions all the more acute.

If you were to try to define the changes of mood which have occurred in Britain since then, as a result of post-war experience, I think you would find three to be most widespread—the realisation that a large centralised government bureaucracy may not be the best managerial answer; that profitability and efficiency are often allied, not opposed; and that the ideal of "fair shares" is even better if there is something to share. Managerial efficiency, profitability, productivity are a new trinity. To a considerable extent, they cut across the old public versus private controversy. Public enterprises need decentralised decision-making. Public enterprises and services must pay their way—which means earning a large enough profit to cover realistic rates of interest and rapid amortisation. All enterprises must press output with all the skill and ingenuity they possess.

I believe this change of mood is appearing in India, although it is held back by ideology, by continuing prejudice, by a lot of misunderstanding and by frequent abuses. Nonetheless, it represents the climate of growth and should be fostered, not impeded. It is perhaps the most important single change needed in the entire industrial structure.

A few illustrations will make the point clearer. I believe there is much more general realisation that Delhi cannot make all the decisions. The attempt has been made to give bodies like the Damodar Valley authority more genuine autonomy.

Decisions are being decentralised, I believe, in the public steel industry. At the same time, there seems to be much more awareness of what good management entails. The belief that a retired permanent secretary can run anything from a fertiliser plant to a penicillin factory has given place to the recognition of skilled management as a scarce and invaluable resource. In any developing economy, manning and managing three giant steel works simultaneously—with private expansion going ahead as well—would have virtually drained the managerial and technical pool. Having discovered this fact the hard way, the Indian government has very sensibly gone about finding more skilled men from outside—from private industry, from abroad if need be.

I believe, too, that profits are ceasing to be a "dirty word" and that their essential economic function of providing the surplus for further expansion is much more widely recognised. Mind you, if Hindustan Machine Tools does so well that it can finance a doubling of its plant out of profits, the result is a "gift to the nation;" if Mr. Mahindra makes profits on the same scale and reinvests them, there will still tend to be murmurs of capitalist exploitation. But at least public corporations are no longer expected to run virtually as charitable agencies, subsidising everyone else.

Having said so much, I feel compelled to add that I do not think the change of mood has gone far enough or that government yet recognises the extreme scarcity and preciousness of really good entrepreneurial talent capable of reaching targets and earning handsome surpluses for reinvestment along the way. In fact, the business world before the emergency seemed more discouraged than at any previous time—more convinced of government hostility, more fearful of being squeezed out, more convinced that no productive achievements on their side could ever change the ideological bias at the Centre.

I think one must hope that some abatement of the ill will can be achieved out of the emergency, out of the experience of further growth. The atmosphere of distrust and discouragement can become a singular disincentive to further growth. I have rarely met any Indian who disputed the "socialistic pattern" or the government's desire to control "the commanding heights of the economy." But many of the men actively engaged in the private sector wish that the value of their work could be less grudgingly assessed. It is a fact that throughout the Plans, private investment has exceeded its target; public investment has fallen short. And in one crucial sector—fuel—government bias has undoubtedly led to absolute shortage.

In the case of the oil industry, a country as short of capital as India might well have left a lot of costly exploration to private companies. There has been nothing but loss to the economy in the delays imposed on the expansion of existing private refineries or of the utilisation of their by-products. With farming in mind, one thinks with particular regret of the fertiliser plant that never got built at Bombay.

The coal record is disastrous—simply because coal enters into everything. The private sector, hampered until recently by unrealistic prices and by prohibitions on any expansion beyond contiguous areas, has nonetheless fulfilled its Plan target. The entire shortfall—of over seven million tons in 1960/61—has occurred in the public sector.

TABLE 4

COAL OUTPUT

(million tons)

	Target 1960	*1960/61*	*1961/62*
Private Sector	44	44.39	45.62
Public Sector	16	10.45	8.73
Total	60	54.8	54.3

Yet, in the Third Plan, this faltering public sector is allotted the bigger rate of increase and a larger share of capital with which to achieve it. Meanwhile, the coal bottleneck is more responsible than any other single factor for the general slowdown which the famous bottlenecks have brought about.

To recognise realities, to encourage the sectors that are meeting their targets, to applaud the earning and reinvesting of profits, to reward efficiency wherever it appears, and castigate it when—as in the big Delhi power breakdown of 1961—it most manifestly does not: all this entails no sacrifice of justice and fair shares. It is perfectly compatible with all sorts of measures to ensure greater equity—by income taxes, wealth taxes, inheritance taxes. In fact, firms might well be fiscally encouraged to make wider experiments in profit sharing and in giving more "fringe benefits"—pensions, in particular, which would give better living conditions without risking inflationary wage increases. Nor does greater recognition of the function and value of efficiency, profitability and productivity wherever they appear affect the socialistic pattern. The "commanding heights" will be largely controlled by government for it alone can provide the needed capital. But a few private groups competitively scaling some of the slopes will strengthen the structure and, perhaps more often than is comfortable, provide a yardstick for measuring the effectiveness of public performance. This is all to the good. What India needs to avoid at all cost is an economy in which neither incentives nor sanctions work. A stagnant economy may achieve fair shares but sharing scarcity is hardly an adequate goal—least of all for a country in which national income is still no more than $70 a head.

3

The Foreign Exchange Crisis

WHEREVER one starts in the effort to disentangle India's difficulties, the thread leads back sooner or later to the shortage of foreign exchange which, in both 1961 and 1962, led to a deficit of the order of Rs. 3,000 million and, at the beginning of 1963, reduced India's reserves to Rs. 2,146 million—or the equivalent of 2½ months' imports. Each of the three ways of securing foreign exchange—foreign aid, foreign investment, or exports—presents problems and none is strictly adequate. This may seem an extreme statement with regard to aid since the AID India consortium of Western Nations under the chairmanship of the World Bank have guaranteed over $2,000 million in aid during the first two years of the Plan.

TABLE 5

WESTERN AID TO THE THIRD PLAN

(million dollars)

	1961/62	*1962/63*	*Total*
Canada	28	33	61
France	15	45	60
Germany	225	139	364
Japan	50	55	105
United Kingdom	182	84	266
United States	545	435	1,000
World Bank			
International	250	200	450
Development Assoc.			
Austria*	—	5	5
Belgium*	—	10	10
Italy*	—	53	53
Netherlands*	—	11	11
	1.295	1,090	2,385

* Joined Consortium in 1962

Source: Official Statistics

But we have to remember, once again, the question of scale. The 450 million people living in India make up a third of the population of the developing world. If aid is judged on a per capita basis, it works out at 30 cents a head—less than aid to Pakistan, much less than aid to Formosa or to some of the troubled successor States of Indo-China. One must assume that the success of an alternative, non-totalitarian method of development is worth something in the worldwide competition with Communism—that competition will continue in the poorer parts of the world whichever version of Communism prevails, pacific or violent, Russian-style or Peking-style. One must assume that the preservation of the open society in Asia has an absolute value for people who claim freedom for their way of life. With such issues at stake, it is not folly or "squandermania" or "pouring good money after bad" to undertake the full support of the Indian balance of payments during the coming years of strain—even if another billion dollars are involved. The costs which some of the possible alternatives might entail—the infiltration of India, the collapse of its economy, its dissolution into warring local dictatorships, a repetition of the Chinese disintegration between the wars—would demonstrably be much higher in the long run or, perhaps, as the Korean War demonstrated, in the not so very long run.

However, one has to admit that the climate for greater aid is not promising. The United States Congress has always felt fairly grudging about spending their electors' money on non-voters abroad. Fear of Communism, dedicated Administration leadership have kept them on the straight and narrow path for a decade. But, as the years go by, a new factor is entering in—a growing desire to see results. The results may be political—warm friends secured for the United States. They may be economic—demonstrably rapid growth. They are usually wholly unrealistic, either because it is always difficult for the poor to love the rich or because the difficulties of early development are simply not understood in wealthy, industrialised countries.

Could more be done to lessen this malaise? I wish myself that aid could be removed from the narrow categories of giving and taking and put into the context of a joint attack on world poverty. It is always an uneasy business—acknowledging debts and being grateful for help, especially when the gratitude can be given all sorts of political overtones. The effusive thanks which some Western donors would like from some Eastern recipients smacks of bending the knee to Western neo-colonialism.[1] In fact, some Indian leaders have felt obliged to go as far as direct discourtesy in order to prove the purity of their non-alignment. Somewhere between these extremes it should be possible to establish reasonable terms for a dialogue which, one must hope, will continue for at least another decade and ought clearly to be less beset with snubs, misunderstandings and hurt feelings. The only context I see in which this might happen would be a joint acceptance of the fact that the misery of so many millions of men and women is a load which the human race should not be asked to carry and that it is as much in the Western interest as in India's to see that, in Lincoln's words, "the burdens are at last lifted from the shoulders of all mankind."

Before leaving the issue of foreign aid, I would like to underline one further point. Even if, for the reasons I have described, an increase in aid-giving, even to counter the emergency, does not prove possible, I think some of the strain could be taken off the Indian economy if more of the aid were not tied to particular projects. Two-thirds of Britain's aid, four-fifths of America's is earmarked for further expansions in productive capacity. Some of the linkages—one thinks of new power stations, for instance—are, no doubt, indispensable. But might not greater flexibility with the rest ensure that more of the existing plant works to capacity before further extensions are planned? Capacity working is the speediest way of increasing the rate of growth. It is, for instance, profoundly disturbing to be told for over two years that the investment has now been made to ensure that the public sector produces its full quota of coal and yet, for two years, to find output static or falling. Investment which leads to 60 per cent capacity working has an element of disinvestment. At the moment, aid in general support of the balance of payments which would permit a larger

[1] Communist aid, which amounts to just under a billion dollars over the last decade, lacks these overtones since Russia never exercised colonial control in India and, so far, is still able to present itself as a proletarian made good, not as a bourgeois.

flow of materials and components to existing factories is India's first need.

The degree to which foreign investment can fill the gap in foreign exchange is not great. Although between 1918 and 1960, foreign business investment rose from Rs. 2,588 millions to Rs. 6,107 millions and, since 1957, the number of agreements for technical and financial participation has increased sharply, the Third Plan's estimate that foreign private investment would not bring in much more than Rs. 60 crores a year is probably not too wide of the mark. India is attractive as a growing market. Its record in the repatriation of profits and capital is impeccable. Compensation is guaranteed in the case of expropriation. Recently, firms pioneering new ventures, have been exempted for a period of years from the very heavy taxation imposed on companies. Yet the malaise which prevails in the Indian government's handling of private enterprise spills over into the foreign sector. On the government side, the distrust has deep historical roots. Much typical nineteenth century investment did amount to exploitation, particularly in the field of minerals, for which the French have coined the phrase *le trouisme*. By this, they mean an investment policy which opens up a lode or a reef, removes the minerals with the help of a wholly foreign supervisory staff, exports the profits, the capital gains and most of the salaries, pays locally only unskilled labour and finally decamps, leaving behind nothing but some unemployed miners and, where the deposit was, *un grand trou*—one large hole. The sense that in foreign investment the entire benefit is exported, dies hard. And the lingering suspicion of exploitation puts an uncertain edge to the welcome given to foreign capital.

Developing governments have therefore to be reminded of three things. The first is that the well-established foreign firm is an incomparable school for skills in the early stages of industrialisation. The proviso is that local staff is trained, but "Indianisation" is universal in private industry in India. The second fact is that foreign capital is scarce and shy. There is more demand than supply and if a government makes its terms too onerous, the capital will not flow. On this point, the Indian government has combined a welcome pragmatism with its sterner attitudes. The proscription of foreign majority holding of shares has been waived in some cases. An investment centre has been established in America to encourage the ventures. Various official credit corporations are prepared for participation. This flexibility somewhat offsets the tough taxation and the "damn'd disinheriting continuance" of some Ministers.

It is especially for these men that the third point needs to be stressed—the degree to which, in the developing countries today, it is the governments, not the companies, that hold most of the cards. So much nineteenth century investment took place in dependent territories without governments of their own. For nearly a century, major economic decisions were in alien hands. In such conditions it is hardly surprising that new governments do not always realise at once what powers political independence gives them and how the relationship of power has changed between the foreign entrepreneur and the local government. What, after all, does a foreign entrepreneur do? He invests his capital and builds his plant; at this point, a solid part of his resources are, as it were, a hostage in the country of his investment. He cannot ultimately control any part of his environment. The government of the country can and does. Of course, if governments go in for indiscriminate, uncompensated takeovers, they probably will not secure any more investment. But this does not help the man who is already in. A truly independent government has powers of control over foreign investment which formerly were either exercised by colonial officials or not at all. The whole context of power has changed. The days of *trouisme* are over.

Independent governments have vast powers of taxation. Since, physically, the plant of the foreign company is in their territory, they exercise ultimate control over conditions of work. They can regulate the speed with which profits and capital are repaid. They can profoundly affect the reactions of the labour force. It is the foreign investor who, once the investment is made, plays from relative weakness. If developing governments fully realised their strength, they could afford to be quite moderate in the way they use it—on the whole. I believe the trend is in that direction.

On the other hand, there are very real difficulties which

foreign enterprise has to appreciate. In the post-colonial world, there cannot be, long-term, a continuance of the Cuban pattern under Batista according to which a country ends up with large parts of key sectors in its economy under foreign control. I would like to see Western firms use all their skill and imagination to devise ways in which foreign investment can become a true and recognisable partnership. There are many routes—joint enterprises, local ownership of shares, participation by the State in private ventures, profit sharing with the local labour force. I think that here, too, the trend is towards greater cooperation, a greater process of getting "mixed up together." Such bodies as the World Bank, the IDA and the various credit institutions set up inside developing countries are all helping to produce a much greater variety of patterns of partnership.

The Indian government itself seems to me to be growing increasingly and sensibly pragmatic about the issue. Let me give a recent example. Back in 1956, under the pressure of the Mysore State government, the Centre felt obliged to nationalise the private Kolar Gold Mining Company. Recently, the Central Provinces Manganese Ore Company fell into a dispute with the state governments of Madhya Pradesh and Maharashtra about the duration of its leases. Once again, the States' reaction appears to have been: nationalise. This time, however, the Centre has persuaded the local governments to enter into a quadrapartite partnership—Centre, Company and the two State governments—to continue the leases. The public authorities bought into the private venture but it controls management and sales.

If governments, confident of their powers, use them reasonably, if private investment recognises the local interest in securing participation in equity and capital gains, agreements profitable to both sides are negotiable. There are some areas—the "commanding heights" again—where any government (including General de Gaulle's) will wish to avoid majority holdings by outsiders. There are some activities—which create neither exports nor import substitutes—in which foreign participation and the resulting repatriation of profits would simply add to the problems of foreign exchange. But, in general, foreign enterprise is an unequalled school of managerial and technical skills, a source of productivity and further savings and, very often, a significant booster of exports as well as an original source of foreign exchange. The test here—as in domestic enterprises—is efficiency and productivity. They are too precious for any source to be overlooked.

The crucial issue in foreign exchange centres, however, on the exports by which India can pay its way. It is only in the last eighteen months that positive steps in export promotion have been taken—the establishment of trade centres abroad, incentives to exporters in such shapes as differential traffic rates at home and the right to retain part of the foreign exchange that has been earned, compulsory setting aside of textile quotas for export, the establishment of a small fund to finance raw materials for exporters. All these measures are too recent and some would say, still too small, to affect exports greatly, and, indeed, far from a six per cent increase a year being registered under the Third Plan, exports have hardly risen at all. It is clear that Rs. 650 crores is some kind of a threshold which it is very difficult to cross.

TABLE 6

GENERAL COMMODITY PATTERN OF INDIAN TRADE

(million rupees)

Domestic exports	*1960*	*1961*	*Imports*	*1960*	*1961*
Tea	1,200	1,244	Non-electric machinery	1,838	2,309
Fabrics other than cotton*	760	840	Iron and steel	1,177	1,022
Cotton fabrics*	585	505	Chemicals	852	890
Fruit and vegetables	246	265	Cereals and preparations	1,796	883
Leather	256	260	Petroleum and products	784	795
Iron ore and scrap	214	248	Raw cotton	753	693
Raw cotton	107	187	Electric machinery	547	635
Tobacco and manufactures	157	158	Transport equipment	669	574
Non-ferrous ores and concentrates	165	134	Copper	229	205
Textile yarn and thread	110	126			

* Excluding narrow and special fabrics.

Source: Monthly Statistics of the Foreign Trade of India.

And the reasons are not in dispute. Over half of India's exports are "traditional"—tea, cotton goods and jute (Table 6). The new manufactured lines suffer severe competition from other Asian producers and from Communist exporters. If at this point it is necessary to go beyond the Indian scene and look at the state of the world market as it affects developing countries, it is simply because, in the field of rising exports, the possibilities do not depend upon countries like India. The scale and scope of the market will be determined largely by the West.

One of the new facts about international trade that has become visible only in the last year or so is the fact that nearly all the trading policies of the developed industrial Western world are in some measure tipped *against* the underdeveloped countries. Science and technology are partly responsible. Development in the chemical industry, substitutes, artificial fibres, plastics, have reduced the nineteenth century dependence of the developed world upon the primary producer. The tremendous impulsion to development in other continents which, a hundred years ago, sprang from the Western countries' hunger for raw materials, has lost much of its energy. Imports grow much more slowly than industrial growth.

From this flows the tendency of primary prices to be very weak in relation to manufactured goods and, therefore, for the terms of trade to turn against the developing world. More and more of their primary products have to be sold to buy a given quantity of manufactured imports. This trend is reinforced by technological developments inside the poorer countries. We have, perhaps, grown accustomed to the image of the American farmer with grain pouring out of his eyes, ears, nose and mouth; we swallow hard and accept the fact that the same farmer is going to reappear in Europe. Over-production of food is no longer a possibility. It is a fact if we only regard market conditions and not real human need.

Owing to the general wealth of America, the American farmer, via a very powerful lobby in Washington, can secure an income commensurate with his needs. The policy creates a vast surplus of food, which, in turn, makes possible such brilliant innovations as the disposal of American food under Public Law 480. But where the primary producers are poor and cannot be subsidised by fellow-citizens as poor as they are themselves, the problem of over-production of such things as coffee, tea, cocoa, groundnuts, rubber and bananas, threatens to undermine still further the incomes of poor countries. The threat is there already. But the reality may be worse. I recently visited some of the research stations of West Africa. In every one of them one would meet some absolutely dedicated scientist who would say, with shining eyes: "Now, with a very simple change in the seedling and a very simple application of fertiliser, we can increase production of these groundnuts—or tea or coffee or rubber—by 1000 per cent." When I said "Oh! but there is a world carry-over of so and so many tons already" the reply was often a blank look: "Is there? But let me tell you more about our methods." Nearly every tropical country has tea, coffee, sugar, groundnuts and rubber written into their development plans. What happens when all these plans, jet-assisted by science, take off together? A further fall in world prices seems the least disturbing of the possible results.

Terms of trade turning against the poor—that is the first problem. The second is that if primary producers try any working-up or processing of their raw materials or minerals before they are exported, the West claps on higher tariffs. The reaction is a clear dis-incentive to the developing world to begin the processing and working up of their own materials which is perhaps the first essential step towards their own effective industrialisation. Then one should add that many tropical products are also subject to excise taxes inside Europe, which tends to keep down their consumption. And we must not forget quotas. In the first stages of development, manufactured exports tend to consist of textiles and simple engineering products. In keeping with the West's anti-processing policy, they invite high tariffs. In addition, if they succeed in penetrating Western markets beyond a certain point, quotas are introduced to protect the higher-cost Western producers.

Nor is it only Western policies that create difficulties. Communist foreign trade is not based upon any definable or observable costing system. A quite usual pattern appears to be to charge 5 per cent less than the nearest competitor. It is difficult to see how the Asian exporter can deal with this problem easily. He does not necessarily have behind him a government ready to give large State subsidies or consumers who will pay much more for goods at home so that they can be sold below cost abroad.

These are general world-wide difficulties. But there is one specific problem that must be examined—the problem of the Common Market. We do not know how soon or even how General de Gaulle's veto on Britain's entry can be overcome. But we have to remember that, whether Britain goes in, or whether Britain stays out, the consequences for the trade of the developing world are likely to be far-reaching. True, 75 per cent of India's trade would not, in fact, be affected because it would have duty-free entry both into Britain and Europe. But in the vital field of textiles, there are bound to be repercussions. If Britain joined Europe, India would lose its preference on textiles and, more than that, Belgian and French producers would receive preference against India. But before anyone throws his hat in the air over the General's veto, he must remember that Indian textile exports to Britain are already limited by quota. If Britain, as a result of exclusion from the Common Market, could not improve on its present rather inadequate 2 to 2.5 per cent rate of growth and if, in 1971, when the changes in tariff would have been completed, British markets had hardly grown, then it is not likely that the quotas would give much greater access to Indian textiles than they do now.

If, to carry speculation rather further, one makes a fairly optimistic assumption about Britain's entry into the Common Market and assumes that Britain, along with the rest of the Common Market countries, would sustain a rate of growth of about 4 or 5 per cent a year, then it is possible that the *total* European textile market would, in fact, be so much bigger that, in spite of the abolition of the preferential system, there would be more openings for Indian textiles than there could be in a restrictive stagnant, though preferential, British Market.

My own belief is that on balance it is to the advantage of the developing world that the French veto should be overcome. Britain has, inescapably, world-wide commercial links with developing countries. The British could not go in and forget all these connections. They would, therefore, tend to reinforce those inside the Common Market who do not want to see it as a sort of private hunting-ground for the French farmer. A British reinforcement to Europe's outward-looking forces could, I think, be strong. Moreover, Britain's entry would render more likely the drawing up of the world-wide agreements we need if we are to deal effectively with all the various issues in world trade—low primary prices, risks of glut, anti-processing tariffs and so forth—which we have just discussed and which add up to an immense barrier to the trade of all the developing nations. Britain in the Common Market would facilitate the kind of agreements with the United States which would be necessary to create new patterns of trade to help developed and developing alike.

What kind of agreements are these? First of all, readiness to back, support and provide, where necessary, the working capital needed to establish world-wide commodity agreements in any area where absolute surplus is becoming a problem. Coffee is already a case in point; tea and cocoa are on the way. Sugar is already included. So are various minerals, with various degrees of success. Such agreements imply discipline among exporters and do run risks of rigidity and monopoly. But the present unregulated market puts all the load on the poorest members.

A second area of agreement might begin with an expansion of the existing textile agreements in such a way that the textile producers in the developing world get a better chance. At the moment, the textile agreement at least represents the first attempt on the part of the developed world to get to grips with the problem. It is based upon quotas which largely reflect the developing countries' exports in the last few years, but with the proviso that the quota will increase by 5 per cent a year for the next five years unless insuperable difficulties occur. A shared loophole is hardly a royal road to further exports. Yet it is nonetheless the first break-through to a recognition that, if the Western world wants to have beneficial trading relations with the developing world, then steadily it has to enlarge its own market to their manufactures. Although the agreement is small, it may be the thin end of the wedge and maybe the wedge will grow bigger. Areas like the American South may perhaps follow Lancashire's pattern which has been to shift out of cheap textiles into quite other fields such as engineering. There has been here a certain "vacation of the field" which one would like to see generalised, the more developed nations moving on to more complex technologies and importing cheaply the simpler technologies which developing countries can most easily make.

Yet agreements such as these depend finally on continued prosperity in the Atlantic World. People do not maintain import prices and "vacate fields" when they are struggling with massive unemployment. The most important factor in maintaining the trade of the developing world will simply be the buoyancy and the expansion of the existing economy. If that economy comprising 200 million people in North America and something nearer 400 millions in Europe and Britain, were able to grow fairly steadily at a rate of 4 per cent a year, this in itself would be the greatest spur to the growth of exports throughout the developing world. It seems to me that this kind of steady expansion is much more likely to take place if there are common institutions linking both sides of the Atlantic, working to keep expansion before the minds of governments, to provide the working capital of international trade and to prevent the problems of the balance of payment from stopping economies dead in their tracks, as Britain has tended to stop every three years since 1947. If the developed world can advance to more institutionalised expansion and prosperity, that would be the best guarantee of buoyant markets and, therefore, of expanding exports for everyone else.

At this point, I would like to underline the degree to which a profound convergence of interests exists between developed and developing lands. It has been a commonplace almost since Marx to point out that the modern industrial economy tends to choke itself in its own productivity. Marx thought exploitation would prevent the workers from ever becoming a market. The vote, trade unions, better technology belied him and, by 1914 quite a lot of Western workers had some stake in the economy. The next great block came in the thirties when even a moderately prosperous working class provided too narrow a market to absorb new technologies and mass unemployment set in.

Then the vast "public works" of the War and the expansion of "consumer durables" created a wholly new market which, in the forties and fifties, enfranchised millions of new consumers round the Atlantic.

Now, in the sixties, the machines are catching up again. America and Britain are stuck with a two per cent growth rate. Western Europe is slowing down. Where is the next stimulus, the next enfranchisement of new consumers to occur? Is it fanciful to suggest that the millions of the developing world could make up the next great extension of the Consumer's Market and that new expansive policies for trade and aid, far from representing self-denial and sacrifice for the West, may be the condition of survival for their mixed market economies?

Seen in this light, a cooperative effort to see India through the emergency, to get a 4 to 5 per cent rate of growth established and to draw 450 million people to the first modest fringes of wellbeing is not a work of charity or condescension or paternalism or even political self-interest. It is a sane answer to the risks—of slump and misery and despair—which could still assail developed and under-developed lands alike. The portents of 1929 are not so wholly banished that the world's statesmen can afford to disregard falling demand among under-developed producers and slackening growth among the developed. Is there not a hint of 1927 and 1928 in the present sense of pause and uncertainty all round the world? Given this context, aid to India is not simply support for the Indian economy. It can be part of a wider strategy, to keep open reasonable hopes and modest perspectives for all mankind.